# KIDS WRITE JOKES

## 100% NONSENSE
## 254% HILARIOUS

Andrews McMeel
PUBLISHING®

Andrews McMeel Publishing
a division of Andrews McMeel Universal
1130 Walnut Street, Kansas City, Missouri 64106

www.andrewsmcmeel.com

Originally published in 2018 by Blink Publishing.

19 20 21 22 23 SHO 10 9 8 7 6 5 4 3 2 1

ISBN: 978-1-5248-5199-6

Library of Congress Control Number: 2019932499

Editor: Katie Gould
Designer: Sierra Stanton
Production Editor: Margaret Daniels
Production Manager: Carol Coe

---

**ATTENTION: SCHOOLS AND BUSINESSES**

Andrews McMeel books are available at quantity discounts with bulk purchase for educational, business, or sales promotional use. For information, please e-mail the Andrews McMeel Publishing Special Sales Department: specialsales@amuniversal.com.

For Molly,
the funniest one of all

# Introduction

Once upon a time, the company I worked for launched a website for kids' jokes, and—fortunately for me—I was given the task of reviewing the jokes that were sent in.

It became clear that children often have a very special view on what constitutes a "joke": they don't have to actually make any sense.

At all.

While I sat there at my desk moderating submissions, I started to realize that a lot of the "incorrect" jokes I was rejecting were actually funnier than the ones I was letting through. Many of them made me laugh out loud in the office. I decided that the world deserved to share in that laughter, and my Tumblr account for Bad Kids Jokes was born.

It didn't take long for the online community to discover the content and, quite frankly, to go a bit crazy over it. And then the press got interested: *The Times*, *Huffington Post*, *Rolling Stone*, Mashable, and BuzzFeed all wrote articles about the site. *The Independent* published a story in the newspaper about it. It was mentioned on BBC Radio. Oh, plus Stephen Colbert and Sarah Silverman read some of the jokes aloud on The Late Show.

Thrilled and amazed by the response, I relaunched the content on Twitter as Kids Write Jokes, and it turns out that tens of thousands of people agree with me that the "jokes" are hilarious.

Why is it so popular? I think it's the fact that every time you read one of these jokes, you picture a young child writing it, convinced and excited that they have something hilarious and amazing to share. The childhood innocence of silly nonsense is universally enjoyable. Sometimes the kids forget that jokes need a punchline. Sometimes they randomly leave out a key point that would have made the whole thing work. And sometimes they forget that a joke needs to be, well, a joke. But to the kid writing it, it makes perfect sense, and that's what's so funny about them and why I love these jokes so much. It's also why I've left each one untouched and unedited—here for the first time in this book in their original form!

I hope you have as much fun reading these as I did compiling them. I still laugh out loud as I read through these pages.

@KidsWriteJokes

why was the naked man naked.
a. he had nakedpower.
b. he had a naked pecan friend.
c. he was naked man.

(james, 8)

A duck walks into a bar. A man runs out because its unnatural to have a duck in a bar.

why the man was naked
a. he was naked guy
b. he had a buttcheek
c. buttoast

(james, 8)

Why do fish have hands?
because they don't have hands

Im going to get to the BOTTEM of this.
HA HA HA HA HA HA HA HA HA HA HA
HA HA HA HA HA HA HA HA HA HA HA
HA HA HA HA HA HA HA HA HA HA HA
HA HA HA HA HA HA HA HA HA HA HA
HA HA HA HA HA HA HA HA HA.

Doctor Doctor I feel like im a curtain

Shut Up

(Arlo)

a man found a raisin in the woods.
"what a funny looking raisin."
"im not a raisin im just an ant
with no legs."

What did the goat say to the dog
nice buttock you loser

KNOCK KNOCK! WHOS THERE.
REX THE DUMPLING EGG

doctor doctor i fell over
get back up then cheese face

what is furry and lays eggs
and also flys?
a hot air chicken egg

doctor: u look look like the
walking dead
man: i just have a cold
doctor: oh yeh, im not a doctor,
im a builder

guess what the chicken was wearing

monkey pants

docter docter i have worms in my garden
i dont care cant you see im busy
you are doing youre nails.

(seth, 8)

What does your mom need to make
her fase very dirtey
SHE needs to go in the trashcan
474844747474747474474747474 times

how meny kicks dus it take to
brake a bed
1000

why did the man scream
his pet chiken pooped on his computer

(holly)

how do you lose four pounds
*cut your hed off*

I have a butt
Sir we all have butts

knock knock
toilet to the rescue

what do you call a donkey with a
millon eyes and a millon legs.
a monster

(rose, 7)

what is crazy and funny
a monkey on a windmill

(melissa)

why did the frog cross the rode?
to get a new tong
why?
because it's tong was stuck to a
velkro tree
how?
the tree was coverd in syrip
what flavor?
mint

# How do you make a potato?
# you make it inside your brain

**LETS SEE WHAT DO WE HAVE HERE
A POOP**

Why does moms get so angry
because when she sends you to your
rhoom she can read a fashion book

If a wookie get shot and
it suvives is it a lucky wookie

Knock, knock
who's there?
Fancy
Fancy who?
Fancy lady, bye I have to go and
shop i need more hats

there was two fish in a tank and
one of the fish said
do you know how to drive this thing
**BECAUSE THE FISH ARE DRIVEING
THE TANK IN A WAR**

what did the floor say to the chair

get off me u fat idiot

if you want to catch a bear in the
winter you cut a hole in the ice then
put peas around it then when he comes
to eat them kick him in the ice hole

Q. Doctor doctor I feel like a spoon
A. well stop looking at spoons

(Harriet!)

what do you call a pig with ears?
dum head

wat do you coll a spider with no legs.
a hairy piece of trash!!!!!!!!!!!!!

Once aponer time
The end
HAHAHAHAHAHAHAH

it was a dark and creepy night
there was a black and white
figure in the forest
**it was a cow**

the duck went into the farmers house

duck: can i have some bread

farmer: no

duck: can i have some bread

farmer: no

duck: can i have some bread

farmer: **FOR THE LAST TIME NO**

i appear once in a second, twice in a month and three times in a year, what am i
dont bother theres no answer.

what do you call a deer with no eyes ears mouth and legs?
**NO I DEER**

(jack)

why was a chiken very cross
with the pig
because he lade 100000 eggs and he
was tired and the pig dident do
the cleaning up.

knock knock
whos there
i eat trash
i eat trash who
give me some money thats who

(ryan)

what do you call a sandwitch
with legs
**bready legs**

**WHAT DO YOU DO IF A DINASUAR**
**LOVES YOU**
**YOU HIDE**

what did the egg say to the other egg?
have a eggsellent day.
i hope you laugh out loud and tell your
friends this joke. if your friends dont
get the joke explain the joke.
**IT WILL BE FUNNY**

what do you call a fish with no legs
a fsh

(Aurora D)

Q. what did the cheese say to the
   moldy cheese?
A. you look unwell i will take you
   to Dr cheese

(josh)

**DINOSAUR JOKE**
**KNOCK KNOCK**
**WHO'S THERE**
**DINO**
**DINO WHO**
**DINOSAUR**

why did the cow stare at the orange
juice for three hours
because it said stare

Teacher: Did you ever hear the story of the orange

Child: No

Teacher: aw too bad

what did the doctor say to
the platypus?
you sir are in quite a pickle

man: waiter how long will
my pizza be?
waiter: not very long. lol

how do you get?
put it in a bag whith water and put
it on the floor

hahahaha
**NOTHING!**

how do you talk to a doctor
in fancy language

waiter do you have frog legs.
no Ive always had ketchup legs
with poop on them.

(olly)

what did the muscleman say
to the tiger

ooooooooooooooooooooooooooooo
ooooooooooooooooooooooooooooooo
ooooooooooooooooo.

a man goes to the doctor and said
"doctor I think I have something
stuck in my throught"
so the doctor said "let's take a x-ray"
(this doctor did not no about spines)
"i see the problem a bone is there"


what dose a acid monster have
for lunch?
a acid sandwich

knock knock
whose there
boiled
boiled who
eggs

What do you call a dinosaur
with no eyes?
Shut up

knock knock
who is there
boss
boss who
boss will you give me some pens

*(m harris, 7)*

doctor doctor i think i am a spoon.
sit on that chair and stop staring.

*(ella bella)*

**WHAT DO U CALL A FREAK HORSE**

**JESSICA**

if you go to the ham contest wat
will the man say
you won last year you are
not alowed

well well well. your JUST IN TIME

Question: What do you call a lady
with marmelade on her head.
Answer: Margret.

why did the chiken running
around screming
because it needed to use the toilot


gess how many snakes there are
13

what do you call a camel with no
bones in his back
a horse

what do you call a monkey
eating keys?
**bonkers**

IGLOO YOUR NOT FUNNY DO
YOU UNDERSTAND

crocodiles might be vegitarians
because when they open their mouths,
we could easily put  in vegetables!

why do old people use a walking stick?
because they like colecting sticks.


what did the orange do in the tree?
orange business

Q: What do you call a dog
   that can walk?
A: A HUMAN.

what do you call a person who is yellow?
a cheese statue

(taylor)

Knock knock
whos there
BOB HUMBUG
Bob Humbug who
naughty bob humbug


docter docter i hit my head
what do you want me to do stupid

the lady went down to the BOTOM
of a mountain
lol

were did the ghost watch tv all night.
in his haunted casle

what do cavemen eat

caves

what do you call a pig that
does kararty
**kararty pig man**

what is funny and has eight legs
a clown

what do spys eat instead
of mcdonalds?
spydonalds

bob: doctor doctor i need
a new but.
doctor: what is it bob.
bob: it has a crack in it
doctor: that is normal bob


what did the rabit say to the goat
hey stop messing up my house

(ben)

mom: there are worms in my plate

waiter: those are sousages

**what do you call a tiger with**

**glasses on?**

**a scientist tiger**

wats the difrent btween a cat
and a frog
thay ony have 10 legs

(rahul, 6)

the pig walked into the shop and
the lady said we dont make types
of meat in this shop

the other day i met a man called smith and i said whats the name of his other leg

WHAT DID THE MAN SAY TO THE CURTAIN WHEN IT KEPT TALKING? SHUT UP LOL

if mr brown lived in the brown house
and mr purple lived in the purple
house who lives in the white house
**the mayor**

What goes on the highway at
90 miles an hour?
a baked bean in a jug

how does a poop get out of the toilet?
somhow

(sammi)

what do you call a vampire
with 2 pants?
double pants

what is yellow black and orange?
a newspaper

what is a thunder cats favrite food?
chips and poop and toilets

this boy went to school, his teacher asked him "whats your name?" the boy said "i don't know." so that day he went to his mother and said "whats my name?" so she said cant you see that im cleaning up!!!

(nandita, 7)

Q) why did'nt the man clime up the mountain

A) because there wasn't a mountain

knock

how there

duck

duck who

chicken legs

what is brown and slow and an animal?
**A BROWN CHIPMUNK OLD GRANNY**

*(isabel, 7)*

what do get when you cross a vampire,
homework and brusel sprouts
i dont know its probalely
super dangerous

(alex, 8)

WHY DID THE BANANA CROSS THE ROAD.
TO FIND BANANA SANTA IN BANANA
LAND WITH BANANA UNDERPANTS

(BETHANY R)

What person just talks and talks and talks

**A TEACHER !!!!**

*(Kaleigh, 9)*

why was the hen walking on its head?

**BECAUSE IT HAD A HEMERGENCY**

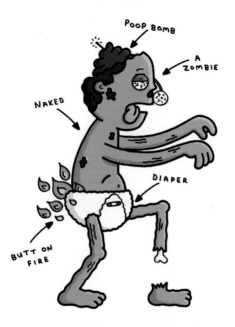

Your brain is a poop bomb and you
are a zombie and you are naked with
your butt on fire and your butt in a
girls face and you are wearing diapers

why did the cow poop on the man?
a man has a toilet but a cow dose'nt.
so a man is a cows toilet


what would you call a man
with no head?
a non head

(matthew, 7)

what do you get when you cross
a centerpede and a pig?
bacon legs

what is the capital of egg.
Milwaukee

(Sara)

Q. whats worse than getting back
   a test with a zero?
A. getting back a test with 100%.
   brag about it. quit from school.
   then find out it wasent really
   yours. you got zero.

# Whats day is March 27........
## St Fartpants Day.

why did tom and jerry get married
Because tom was a boy and jerry was
a boy and they were strong
as a toliet.

WHY WAS THE NINJA IN
THE KITCHEN?
YOU TELL ME!!!!!!!!!!!!!!!!!!!!!

whats round fat and is sticky
**a greedy bee**

do you know one man asked his
son to bring eggs
but he broght apples

(nath, 6)

300 + 5967 - 400 + 20 = head ake

why did the chicken marry
the crocodile
because crocodooladoo is good
family name.

whats ugly but happy
a frog

Why does the chef always
be right........
Because he's the chef.

what do you call a deer with no eyes
EYE dunno

(sam, 7)

What is the secret ingrediant
of a toilot?
Poop

why did the cow go to the movies?
because movies

what makes a super hero fly?
hero dust. boring right

**WHERE DO CHIKENS GO AT
THE WEEKEND
THE MOVIES**

your a trashcan
no Im not
you look like one
ok I am

How do you get a tissue to dance?
You put a little boogie in it
(DONT TRY THIS AT HOME ANYBODY)

What does A friendly neighbor do to you?
1. Buy you a playStation 4.
2. He does'nt care when your stealing.
3. He gave you his credit card.
4. He's kind but he got nothing now.

what did the man do with time
wasted it

How do you hire a teddy bear?
Put him on stilts!
(if you don't get it hire as make tall
if you still don't get it sorry for the
inconvenience)

(Jackson, 9)

where do cows go on vacation
FRANCE

what is the best part of bread......
bread

what do call when two circles are
next to each other.
a butt

monkey joke
q: what keys cant you play
on a piano
a: a monkey


What did the flashlight say
to the car?
Stop it i am changing

Doctor doctor! I feel cold!

Then pull yourself togever man

(Lukas H)

why did mr potateo run from the cops?
because he killed mrs carrot face and
robbed mr broccili pants.

Why does my uncle Kevin
have a run everyday
because he wants to have
a bit of "me" time

what has eight legs eight
heads and 8 arms
= 8 men

hello yes this is a prank call
madam you have won 200,0000,000,00
million dollars!


knock knock
who is there
doctor smelly feet.

what's green and hangs off trees

**GIRAFFE**

why did the banana go
to the doctors?
why?
because he had kechup on he,s head.

What is pink, white and sits in corners while having pizza stuck on the top layered part of the skeleton protecting it outside?
A baby rat in a bag of salt with hot cheese on it's face!

why did the lady put ham in
her hand bag?
because someone told her it was
a ham-bag.

A man of the chicken layed a egg
on a pointy mountain. There was a
big wind and the egg rolled down.
Where did the egg Fall?
The man of the chicken does
not lay eggs!!!

why did the potato cross the road
to get to the mailbox

Dad what is the square root of 144?

WHO CARES!!?? YOU'RE GROUNDED!!!

why did the lion eat the snake
**because it looked like a sausoge**

Q: why do bees have black stripes
A: they live in the dark

(ava, 8)

what did a bee say to a other bee?
i love plants

why did the turkey go on the plane
to go to turkey

*(ffion, 7)*

what do you call a fish with no tail?
a one eyed grape

why didn't the skeleton go swimming
because his eyeballs will be filled
with water

Q. Why are Zombies fast
A. To catch the bus

what has 3 eyes 6 legs and 2 noses
a Cyclops goat with a man wearing
a animal suit breeding

What did the chicken say to the pilot?
Can I have a ride to chicken island.


Waiter waiter why is there
a foot on my cake
Because you told me to stomp on it

docter docter I feel like a bunch
of curtans
then open them up

(marla, 7)

why is the mash potato not cool?
Because it isnt wearing sun glasses.

**WHAT DOES A MONKEY KEEP
AS A SECRET
THAIR BANANAS**

what's a jedi's favorite food?
lightsaber casserole

Knock,Knock......
Who's There?.....
The Big Bad Wolf......
What Do You Want?.......
Colored EGGS......
What color?.......
RED!!!!!!!!!!!!!!!!!!!!!!!!!!!!!!!

WHAT DOES PEAS EAT?
TOAST

Father: Shut up! Don't tell your father how to manage our business. I have eaten more salt than you have rice

why shoudnt you go to the fridge
without permition
because it will come for its revenge

"docter docter IVE EATEN TOO MUCH
TRASHCAN SURPRISE"
"DONT TALK BULONY"

knock knock
who's there
the guy who works all day
the guy who works all day who
i wake up i shower i go to work
i work all day i go home i sleep

A MAN ALWAYS LAUGHING HIS NAME
IS WILLSON. 1 DAY A FREIND OF
WILLSON ASK HIM:WHY YOU ALWAYS
HAPPY? WILLSON LOOK HIM FREIND
AND SLAP HIM FREIND AND THAT
DAY WILLSON NEVER LAUGH BECAUSE
WILLSON IS GHOST NOW

What do you call a fish with no eyes
fishhhhhhhhhhhhhhhhhh

A guy was at a store he brought
dome lobsters and said to the man:
AAAAAGH its a crab. And the other
man said thats nota crab its a orange
pencil.

what do you say when somethig
carnt fly?
can it fly yet